10 WAYS TO DEVELOP CHARACTERS

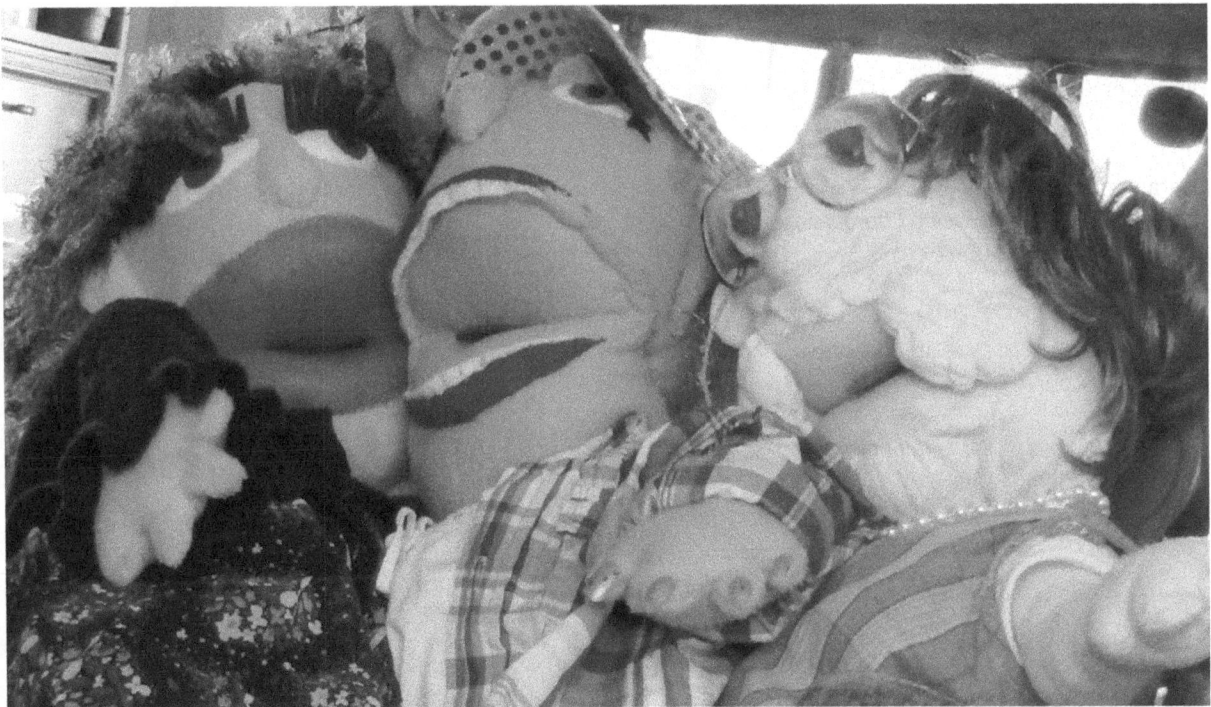

Connie Dunn

ISBN-13: 978-0692210543
ISBN-10: 0692210547

9 8 7 6 5 4 3

Library of Congress

Dunn, Connie
        10 Ways to Develop Characters

Character Development
        10 Ways to Develop Characters
        by Connie Dunn

Characters
        10 Ways to Develop Characters
        by Connie Dunn

Writing
        10 Ways to Develop Characters
        by Connie Dunn

Table of Contents

What Is Character Development.. 5

Archetypes 9

Character Sketch 13

Character Arc 39

Character Secrets 49

Making Characters Real 53

Roles and Character 57

Character and Point of View 59

Character and Plot 63

Character Development and Troubleshooting............................ 67

About Author 71

Many Thanks to Donna Winters
for her proofreading and corrections.

What Is Character Development?

The art of character development can often be the key to writing a good story. If your readers cannot identify with your main character, then it is likely that they will not continue reading.

Characters can be developed by the author in several ways outside of the "story:"

- Through the exploration of archetypes;
- Creating a character sketch for each of your characters;
- Developing character arc or following how the character grows and changes from the beginning of the story to the end;
- Giving your character secrets;
- Adding reality qualities to your characters;
- Building characters to fit the roles in your story;
- Determining how your character fits with your point of view;
- Developing your character so that he or she moves your plot along; and
- Troubleshooting bad characters or more exact: characters that don't work.

However, within a story, you have to develop that character all over again. All the character sketches and arcs and other aids that help you use to develop a well-rounded character outside your story are wonderful aids, but they don't tell the reader who a character is. In most novels, you have more than one character. The main character may be the predominant character, but is not the only character within most stories.

Because the reader only knows what you have written inside that story, you, the author, have to convey who each of your characters are through description and dialogue. Revealing your character slowly helps the reader absorb who the character is. Unfortunately, describing the character is one of the most boring ways to let the reader see who your character is.

When people talk about the art or craft of writing, they usually are speaking about the writing style. It also speaks to how you handle developing the character. Whether your character is the main character or a minor character, the reader cannot see what is not written on the pages.

Some of the things that readers need to know are:

1. **Physical attributes:** What does this character look like? Is this character, tall, short, thin, fat, bald, deaf, or blind?
2. **Environment:** Where does this character live? Does he/she live in a house, a castle, or an abandoned island?
3. **Associates:** Who are the other characters that surround your character? Who are his/her friends, enemies, acquaintances?
4. **Vocation:** What does this character do? Is he/she in school, work, etc,?
5. **Personality:** How does he/she talk, walk, and think? What flaws does this character have?
6. **Emotions:** Is this character strong or weak? How does this character feel about things, such as humanity, life, or death?
7. **Opinions:** Does this character have strong or weak opinions? Does he/she voice these opinions? To whom? Why?

And though we may know the answers to all of this, it has to be communicated to the reader. Nobody wants to read pages and pages of description, so we have to craft this information carefully. For example:

The man wore a red hat and a red tuxedo with a white ruffled shirt. He was 34 and on his way to his wedding in the city. He had never worn such fancy clothes. He was more comfortable on his tractor, wearing overalls and a large sun hat.

Or…

"Hello," said a man wearing a red hat and a red tuxedo with a white ruffled shirt. "I'm looking for St. Joseph's Presbyterian Church. Can you help me?"

The woman directed him to walk down the next street to the right. The Church would be on the left.

"Thank you," said the man, wondering how his bride was going to like the quiet farm life.

In the two examples above, there was information delivered about the character without giving line after line of description. While this is probably not award-winning text, the purpose was to give an example. I'm hoping that it helps you understand how to work in descriptive information.

Archetypes

What are archetypes? That's a good place to begin.

Archetypes are somewhat stereotypical models of people. Archetypes are used in psychology as a method of categorizing behavior. In fiction writing, we categorize different characters through a similar modeling.

Seven Basic Archetypes include:

1. The Teacher;
2. The Wounded Healer;
3. The Leader;
4. The Oracle;
5. The Storyteller;
6. The Innovator; and
7. The Artist.

However, don't get too comfortable with this seven, because there are many others, such as:

1. The Willing Hero;
2. The Reluctant Hero;
3. The Anti-Hero;
4. The Trickster;
5. The Knight;
6. The Sage;
7. The Dark Sage;
8. The Angel;
9. The Clown, Fool, or Jester;
10. The Entertainer;
11. The Guardian;
12. The Seeker or Wanderer;
13. The Judge;
14. The Oracle;
15. The King;
16. The Queen;
17. The Mother or Earth
18. The Sidekick;
19. The Pioneer or Pilgrim; and
20. The Victim.

William Shakespeare popularized the use of archetypes. Writers use archetypes to develop characters, and while the lists above are a good place to start, there are thousands of possibilities.

What writers have to remember is that archetypes are like shell characters or two-dimensional characters. Archetypes are a good place to start, but to create three-dimensional characters; you have to add the human connection, emotion, and whatever else needs to be there to make a well-rounded character.

Archetypes also help authors identify the role a character might play, which ultimately gives you the character arc (see the section on Character Arc for more information) that it might follow. Writers have literally been using archetypes for thousands of years, because readers like the familiar. What I mean by that is that heroes are easily identified and they usually follow certain developments – plots. The hero in the story is known as protagonist. For example, when we think of villains, we have some general ideas about what a villain is going to do. Some people use the term "evil," but perhaps a better description of a villain is the opposite of the hero. The villain is also known as the antagonist.

Let's also remember that good characterization is really what readers want. While starting with archetypes, it's really what we add to that archetype that endears the character to the reader. Readers who identify with the characters are going to return to read other books you write.

While characterization is very important in developing an archetype into a real character, what you have to remember is not to get bogged down in the back story. Don't get me wrong, the back story is important in understanding your character, but the reader doesn't want to go there!

We often hear the term: the character is "flat." That's what I referred to as a two-dimensional character. The character is not a cartoon "flat" as one that has been flattened by something. Nor can you just blow a little air into your character to make them three-dimensional or a "round" character.

In life, we rely on archetypes to help us figure out who we are. We might examine the gods and goddesses of ancient cultures for their archetypes. What woman wouldn't want to examine Aphrodite? What man wouldn't want to examine Thor? Today, we might refer to Aphrodite as "sexy," and Thor might be described as "strong."

Naturally, when we are using archetypes, we have to be aware that these are stereotypes. We have a responsibility in using stereotypes, because we can continue racism, ageism, socio-economical differences, gender identity as a binary system, and many others. There are legitimate reasons for our characters to be the stereotype, but we need to be aware of the impact of using a stereotype. More often, we start with a stereotype and modify the personality, which then takes it out of the stereotypical mode.

I believe where writers fall into trouble with archetypes or stereotypes is when they are trying to create a character that they don't know well, or when they have a character that makes it easy to choose the stereotype instead of building a character that is placed in a stereotypical role.

Let's take a look at a stereotypical role. This is 2014 and "12 Years a Slave" has just left the theatres. The "Butler" in this movie was thrust into a stereotypical role, but the character wasn't stereotypical.

I hope that learning a bit about archetypes enlightened you; and, hopefully, it helps you develop your characters!

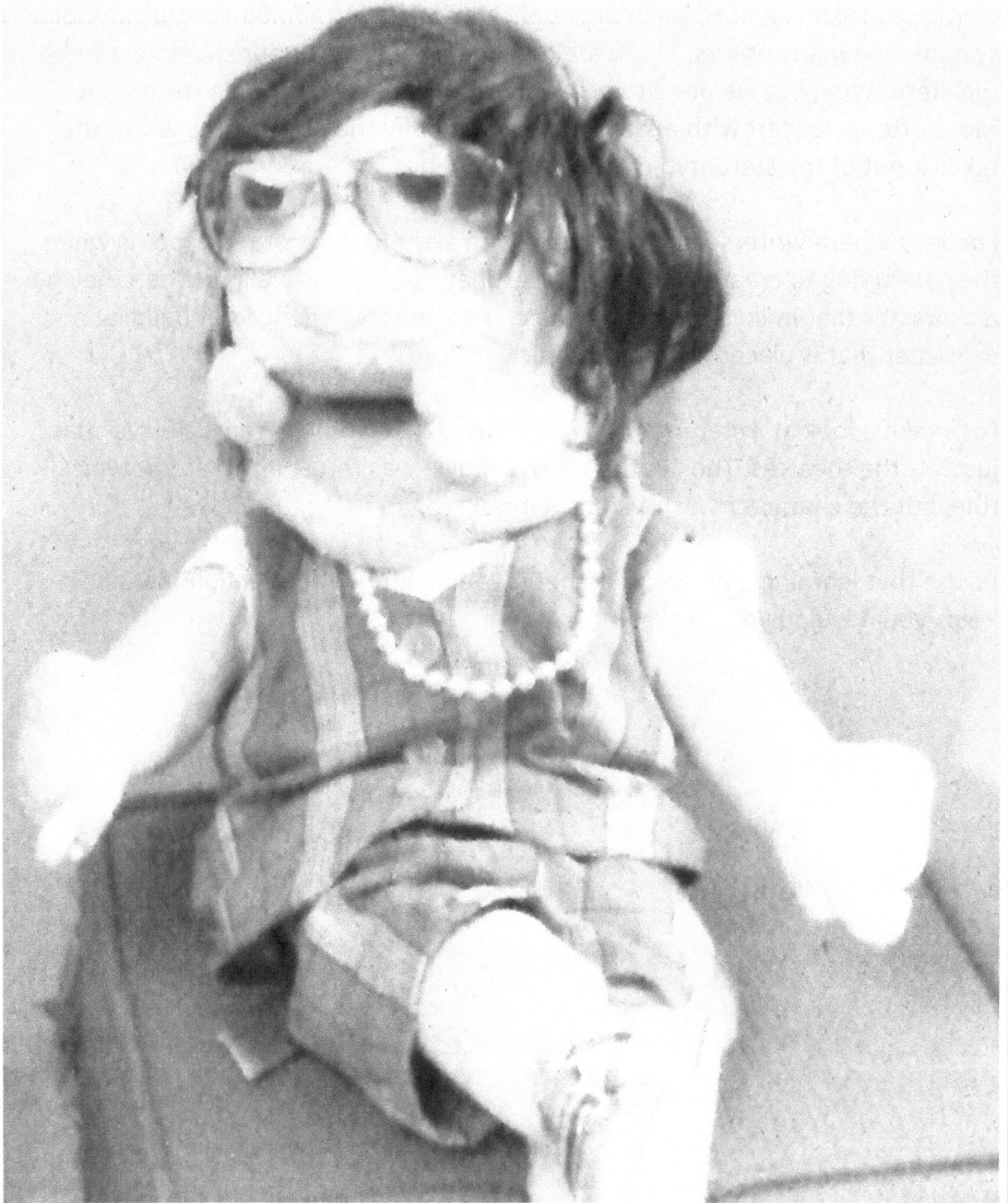

Character Sketch

A *Character Sketch* is a way for you, the writer, to develop your character and his/her back story. The better you know your character; the better you will be able to put your character into your plot and make it feel real. The key to developing any character is to make them someone who your reader can identify with. They have to feel strongly about the character to see what happens next.

We've all gone to the movies or read a book and at the end you didn't feel connected to the story, because the character was just not anyone you could identify with. You don't have to like a character to get sucked into what will happen, but it helps. The best scenario is when you have a hero that you feel so close to that it feels like you are in the story. Then when the villain of the story does things to the hero, you feel strongly about that character in a negative way.

Even if you don't like the villain, he/she is often memorable simply because you felt the character was real. Combine that with identifying with the hero and you have a winner of a story! So no matter what the plot is, if your characters are not well-developed characters no one will be able to feel what they are feeling within the story.

Using a Character Sketch is only a tool. Once you've used this tool to develop you character and his/her back story, you still have to show your reader who this character is within the dialogue and descriptive prose.

This chapter has three different *Character Sketch Surveys*, you don't need to use all three. Pick the one that you feel works best for your book project, your character or that you simply like the best.

Character Sketch Survey - 1

Character Name:
Book Project:
Date:

1. What are your character's physical attributes?

    a. What color is his/her hair?

    b. What color are her/his eyes?

    c. What gender (male/female) is your character? What sexual preference, if applicable?

    d. Does he/she have any distinguishing facial features, such as scars, dimples, etc.?

    e. How tall is your character?

    f. Does your character have a distinguishing walk (such as a limp)?

    g. What sort of clothing would your character wear?

2. How does your character act?
    a. What does your character do for a living/type of school (grade, private/public, etc.)?

    b. Is your character honest or dishonest? How can we tell that?

3. Is your character more of a hero or villain? Why?

4. You can often tell a lot about a character by how he/she spends her/his time.

   a. Does your character have any hobbies? What are they?

   b. When your character is not at school/work, what does he/she spend most of her/his time doing?

4. Miscellaneous attributes. What else do you know about your character?

Character Sketches are one of the best ways to develop your character and their back story. However, if this seems complicated, there are software packages that make this easier to handle. One package that I've used is "Character Writer," which can be found at http://www.characterpro.com/characterwriter/index.html. ***Please note:*** *I do not make a commission on selling this software.*

Character Sketch Survey- 2

Character Name:
Book Project:
Date:

General

1. What makes your character heroic?

2. Describe your characters interaction with people and social events.

3. What are the attributes that your character will add to your story?

4. Why is this character going to be in your story?

5. How does your character interact with the plot?

Personal

1. What is your character's full name, and what name does he/she go by?

2. If your character uses a nickname, what is it and from where did it come?

3. What does your character look like? What is his/her height; weight; color of eyes, hair, skin tone; and age or apparent age? Describe other items, such as tattoos, apparent scars, and other features including facial shape and hairdo.

4. What is the usual dress of this character, such as skirt vs pants; or suit/dress vs casual? How would you describe the normal clothing worn by this character?

5. When this character is "dressed up," what does that look like?

6. When this character is just hanging with the peeps at home or at other locations, how does he/she dress?

7. As your character prepares for bed, what is she/he putting on or taking off?

8. Does your character wear jewelry? Describe the style of jewelry.

9. What is your character's best feature?

10. What is your character's birth date? How does your character feel about his/her age?

11. Where does your character live? Describe it: Is it messy, neat, avant-garde, sparse, etc.?

12. What kind of car does your character drive? Describe it: Is it a fancy car, like a Lexus; sporty, like a convertible; old, like in falling apart?

13. What does your character believe is his/her most prized mundane possession? Why does he/she value it so much?

14. If your character could pick one word to describe him/her, what would it be?

Family

1. What is your character's family structure?

2. What is your character's father like? What is the relationship between your character and his/her father?

3. What is your character's mother like? What is the relationship between your character and her/his mother?

4. How would your character describe her/his parents' marriage? For example, were they married; did they remain married, never married, or divorced.

5. Describe your character's siblings? How many, etc.

6. What is the relation between your character and his/her siblings? Include the worst thing one of his/her siblings did to your character and the worst thing your character did to his/her siblings.

7. When was the last time your character saw a family member and where are they now?

8. How was your character involved with extended family? How did he/she meet these family members, who were they, and what did your character think of them?

Childhood Questions

1. Describe your character's first memory.

2. What was your character's favorite:
   a. toy?

   b. game?

3. What people are important to this character including family and friends?

4. When your character was growing up, who was his/her best friend?

5. What is your character's fondest childhood memory?

6. What is your character's worst childhood memory?

Adolescent Questions

1. At what age did your character go on his/her first date?

2. What is your character's view of authority? Was this formed in adolescence? If so, what was the event that helped solidify this view?

3. When your character was in high school, with what group did he/she hang out?

4. As a high school student, what were your character's goals? What events help form these goals?

5. When your character was an adolescent, who was his/her idol?

6. As your character was growing up, who did she/he fantasize about?

7. As an adolescent, what was your character's favorite memory?

8. As an adolescent, what was your character's worst memory?

Occupational Questions

1. Did your character have a job? What was it? Did she/he like it? If no job, from where did your character's money come?

2. What is your character's boss or employer like? (Or publisher, or agent, or whatever.)

3. What co-workers get along with your character?

4. Why did your character get along with this particular character(s)?

5. Your character had to learn something that he/she hated. What was it?

6. Was your character a spender or saver of money? Why?

Likes & Dislikes

1. What hobbies did your character have?

2. Who were your character's closest friends? Describe them and how your character related to them.

3. Who were your character's worst enemies? Describe these people and why your character didn't get along with them.

4. What sorts of music does your character like? How involved in favorite bands, etc. did your character get?

5. How into music is your character? Is there a tape, CD or MP3 favorite that hasn't left your character's player since your character purchased it? Why?

6. Does your character have a favorite song? What is it? Why?

7. What is your character's favorite movie? Why?

8. What are your character's favorite books? Why?

9. What are your character's favorite Television shows? Why?

10. Is your character interested in politics? Why or why not? If interested in politics would he or she vote?

11. Where does your character hang out with friends? Why?

12. Who are the people that your character hangs out with?

13. What annoys your character? Why?

14. What would be the perfect gift for your character? Why?

15. What's the most beautiful thing your character has ever seen? Why?

16. What is your character's favorite time of day? Why?

17. What type of weather does your character like? Why?

18. What is your character's favorite food? Least favorite food? Why?

19. What is your character's favorite drink? (Coffee, Coke, Juice, Beer, Wine, etc.) Why?

20. Does your character have a favorite animal? What? Why?

21. Does your character have any pets? What are they? What is the relationship?

22. What kinds of things does your character do to get calm and relaxed?

23. What habits do others have that annoys your character?

24. Does your character get embarrassed? What things embarrass him/her? Why?

25. Name the things that your character doesn't like about himself/herself?

26. Describe how your character would like to look.

Sex & Intimacy

1. Does your character consider himself/herself as straight, gay, bi, or something else? Why?

2. Who was the first person your character had sex with? When did it happen? What was it like? How well did it go?

3. Has your character ever had a same-sex experience? Who with, what was it like, and how did it go?

4. What is your character's deepest, most well-hidden sexual fantasy? Would you ever try it?

5. What was the wildest thing your character has ever done, sexually? Who was it with and when did it happen?

6. Are there any sexual activities that your character enjoys and/or practices regularly that can be considered non-standard? (Bondage, Fantasy Play, etc.) Why does your character like it?

7. Are there any sexual activities that your character will not, under any circumstances, do?

8. Does your character currently have a lover? What is his/her name, and what is their relationship like? What are they like as a couple? Why is your character attracted to him/her?

9. What is the perfect romantic date for your character?

10. Describe the perfect romantic partner for your character.

11. Is your character married? If no, does your character ever want to get married? What about children? Is there a timetable?

12. What does your character find more important - sex or intimacy? Why?

13. What was your character's most recent relationship like? Who was it with? (Does not need to be sexual, merely romantic.)

14. What's the worst thing your character has done to someone he/she loved?

Drug & Alcohol

1. Does your character take drugs or drink alcohol?

2. At what age did your character first take drugs? What drugs? What was that experience like for your character? Is your character still taking drugs? Explain fully.

3. At what age did your character first get drunk? What was the experience like for your character? Is your character still drinking? Is he/she an alcoholic or simply a social drinker?

4. Did anything good come out of the alcohol or drugs? Did anything bad come out of it?

5. Does your character continue to drink alcohol or take drugs on a regular basis?

6. What does your character think of drugs and alcohol? Are there people in his/her life who should not drink alcoholic beverages or take drugs? Why or why not?

Morality Questions

1. What is your character's morality?

2. Describe one thing, one act, that your character did in his/her past that he/she is most ashamed of?

3. Name one thing that your character did in the past that he/she is most proud of?

4. Did your character have an argument? With whom? Over what? Who won?

5. Did your character ever get in a physical fight? Over what? With whom? Who won?

6. What does your character feel most strongly about?

7. Does your character ever pretend to feel strongly about something just to impress someone? What does he/she feel strongly about? Who does he/she try to impress? What is the outcome of such behavior?

8. What trait does your character find most admirable? How often does he/she find this trait? Which people in your character's life exhibit this trait more often?

9. What does your character believe should not be incorporated into the media or art (sex, violence, greed, etc.) Why or why not?

10. What disturbing feelings does your character have? Why?

11. What are the spiritual beliefs of your character? What religion, if any, does your character call his/her own?

12. Does your character think the future is hopeful? Why or why not?

13. Is an ounce of prevention really worth a pound of cure? Which is more valuable? Why does your character feel this way?

14. From the Point of View of your character, what's the worst thing that can be done to another person? Why?

15. What does your character believe is the worst thing you could actually do to someone you hated?

16. Is your character a better leader or follower? Why or why not?

17. What is your character's responsibility to the world, if any? Why do you think that?

18. Does your character think redemption is possible? If so, can anyone be redeemed, or are there only certain circumstances that can be? If not, why does your character think nothing can redeem itself?

19. Is it okay for your character to cry? Why or why not? When was the last time your character cried?

20. What does your character think is wrong with MOST people, overall? Why?

Post-Supernatural Awareness Questions

1. What caused your character to become supernatural? What was it like (in your character's opinion)?

2. Now that your character is supernatural, is it good? Why or why not.

3. Does your character have mentors? Who are they? How did your character become their student?

4. Does your character practice white/good or dark/evil magic? Why?

5. If your character is practicing white magic, does he/she practice it with others? Who are these other characters? What is the relationship with your character?

6. If your character is practicing dark magic, does he/she practice it with others? Who are these other characters? What is the relationship with your character?

   a. Think of a major event that happened during your character's training/initiation. What was it? And how has it shaped your character?

   b. What is something your character had to learn during her/his training that she/he hated? Why did your character hate it?

Miscellaneous Questions

1. Is your character frightened of things? What sorts of things? Are there other things even scarier? What does your character think those scarier things would be?

2. Has your character known anyone to die that he/she cared about? In what way did that person/animal die and how did it make your character feel?

3. Has your character ever been injured? What was the worst injury? How did it happen? How did it affect your character?

4. Is your character ticklish? Where? To what degree?

5. Does your character have any long term goals? What are they?

6. Does your character have any short-term goals? What are they?

7. Does your character have any bad habits? What are they? Does your character intend to get rid of those habits? In what way? How do these habits shape your character's life? Do they limit it? If so, how?

8. Is your character famous or ordinary? How has that shaped his/her life?

9. What is your character's occupation/job/career? How does this affect your character?

10. How does your character spend his/her free time?

11. What time period is your character living in? What time period does your character wish he/she lived in? Why? (This is not about changing history.) How would this appeal to your character? And how does the current or wished for time period affect your character?

12. Is your character a private person? Why? If your character is not private, how does that affect his/her life and what caused this to happen?

13. If your character gains an obscenely large sum of money (via an inheritance, a lawsuit, a lottery, or anything else) what would he/she do with it?

14. Let's say your character found a genie, what would be the three wishes he/she would ask for? (Genies do not grant wishes to add more wishes.)

15. When your character gets bored, what does he/she do?

16. If your character had a handicap, what would be the most frightening sort for your character? Why?

17. If your character became disfigured due to an accident or illness, what would be your character's worse nightmare? Why?

Character Sketch Survey - 3

Character Name:
Book Project:
Date:

1. **Appearances:**
   a. What gender is your character?

   b. What does your character look like?

   c. Is your character gorgeous or handsome? How does this affect him/her? Does your character identify with being gorgeous or handsome?

   d. Does your character have any obvious physical flaws or features?

2. **Relationships:**
   a. Are there friendships? Male or female? Is this significant?

   b. How does your character relate to family and friends?

   c. Is your character among the very social? Reclusive? Somewhere in between? Why?

   d. Since people are often defined by those with whom they associate, how does your character rate?

3. Ambitions:

    a. Is your character ambitious? Why or why not?

    b. What does your character feel is his/her passion n life?

    c. What goal(s) is your character is trying to accomplish?

    d. What unrecognized, internal need does your character have? How will he/she meet this need?

4. Character Defects:

    a. What personality trait does your character have that his/her friends or family find:

        i. Too self-centered?

        ii. Too competitive?

        iii. Too lazy?

        iv. Too compliant?

        v. Too demanding of others?

        vi. While you want your reader to like your character (hero, in particular), what other flaws does your character have? (This is often connected to an unrecognized need, which may get resolved through the character arc.)

5. Thoughts:

    a. What kind of internal dialogue does your character have?

    b. How does your character think out his/her problems and dilemmas?

    c. What are the differences or sameness between your character's internal voice and external voice?

    d. How do these create internal conflict?

    e. While in real life, we don't get the benefit of knowing someone else's innermost thoughts, how will you, the writer, use this to your advantage?

6. **The Everyman Quality:**
    a. How does your character relate to others?

    b. What special powers or training does your character have (such as James Bond, Spiderman, or Harry Potter) that makes it hard for the ordinary person to relate?

    c. How can you overcome these special qualities to make your character someone your readers can relate to or aspire to be?

7. **Restrictions:**

a. Your character may have a personality flaw, but he/she may also have a physical or mental weakness that your character will need to overcome in the *Character Arc*. What is this weakness? For example, Superman had his Kryptonite. Spiderman and Batman were human and could be killed.

b. What weakness does your character have that makes him/her more human and better able to relate to readers?

8. We know that the goal is to make our character endearing to the reader and to have your readers *feel* something for your character. How will you add character qualities to your character that will invoke emotion from your readers?

The more emotions your readers have, the more they care about your character; and therefore, the more these readers invest in the story. Perhaps, this is the secret.

Character Arc

A character arc is basically the journey of a character from where they start out in a story to where they end up. For example, John starts out in a story as just some guy, then things happen to John, but John continues on the journey, while enduring many tragedies. There are lots of twists and turns in the story, and John changes because of these.

Many people like to physically graph out the arc. That is one way to see the changes in the character. In a novel, there may be more than one character that changes through the events in the story. They likely don't follow the same arc. There is a lot written about the Hero's Journey, which often is equated with the character arc of the main character. But not everyone sees the main character following the Hero's Journey in every story.

Veronica Sicoe (http://www.veronicasicoe.com/blog/2013/04/the-3-types-of-character-arc-change-growth-and-fall/), science fiction writer, said, "The main reason I disagree with people who claim every story fits the hero's journey, is that it's not the only character arc out there, and it really doesn't fit every story."

Veronica goes on to name three common character arcs: 1) the change arc (typical hero's journey); 2) the growth and shift arc (typically fast-paced thriller, adventure, romance, novels, horror, and science-fiction.); and 3) the fall arc (typically a tragedy).

The change arc is very popular. We can easily understand this arc, because our lives are full of change. Natural growth brings out change. In fact, change is really all there is in our lives. Children change constantly; just ask any parent who has to keep up with clothing their child.

The Change Arc

Looking at the Change Arc is pretty much looking at a real arc in the character development. In the very beginning of your story, the character is one way.

However, by the end, your character is different. A change or transformation has taken place.

Example: *A Spider, Some Thread, and a Labyrinth Walk, $15, published by Nature Woman Wisdom Press* (*http://www.amazon.com/gp/search/ref=as_li_qf_sp_sr_tl?ie=UTF8&camp=1789 &creative=9325&index=aps&keywords=A%20Spider%2C%20Some%20Thread%2C %20and%20a%20Labyrinth%20Walk&linkCode=ur2&tag=publwithconn-20*).

In this collection of stories, there is *"Bramble of Pincup Springs,"* where Bramble is a mere garden spider spinning her web outside the stained glass church window. The groundskeeper was new and didn't know that Bramble had been spinning her webs there for quite some time. He unhinged one end of her beautiful web that she had been working on all morning. Bramble yelled at the man. Bramble's voice was way too quiet for a human to hear. Bramble asked her great, great, great, great, great-grandmother, who was the Spider Grandmother of Native American lore, to grant her a *miracle*. And so she did: it was Easter Sunday and Bramble could speak to humans.

In this story Bramble's arc went from mere garden spider to a super-hero spider who could talk to humans to work out inter-species issues, such as respecting a web of a spider.

The Script Lab (http://thescriptlab.com/) describes the *Change Arc* as the *Hero's Journey*. The *Hero* or the *Main Character* wants something badly (this is the main goal), but is having trouble reaching it due to *Obstacles*.

Darcy Pattison (http://www.darcypattison.com) explains, "In the *Hero's Journey,* a character gets a *Call to Adventure* that takes him/her out of the normal and ordinary world into a world where they must quest for something. One of the key moments in this paradigm is the *Inmost Cave* where the character faces his deepest fears."

Juliet Wade (http://talktoyouniverse.blogspot.com/) says, "Over the course of the story my protagonist has to go from being a bigot to learning to accept others. My character believes in the status quo, but when he finds out about X, he has to accept that the status quo has always been a lie."

"This is what I do a lot," says Juliet, "because a lot of my stories are about people changing their minds, or learning what the key to understanding is, etc. I go very psychological in my stories. If you're doing something similar, take a look at that change that needs to happen, and try to break it down into smaller components. The bigger the change, the more different conditions will have to be in effect for it to happen. If my bigot must change his mind, then he probably needs to be put in an extreme situation where only a member of his despised group can help him, and that person becomes a friend/exception as a result. But there will be many things that need to happen in order to create an extreme situation like that - and many things that must happen thereafter, once the bigot has actually engaged with the despised person, to solidify his impression and expand his doubts about his previous views into a broader personal change."

Perhaps, the *Change Arc* is the easiest of all the *Character Arcs* to identify in stories. It is also the most well-known character arc, as well. The transformation is pretty drastic, which is very compelling to most writers.

The Hero's Journey has been documented heavily. There are many variations of it. I chose the following points:

- Protagonist Faces Problem
- Call to Adventure
- Beginning of Transformation
- Meet Mentor/Helper
- Revelation
- Transformation
- Atonement
- Return to Home

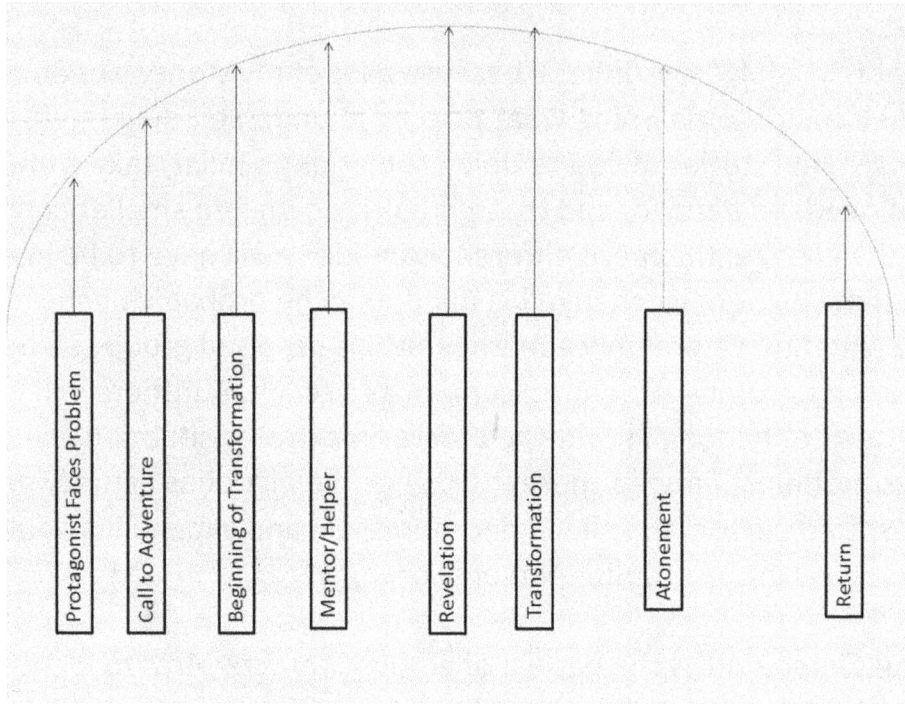

The Hero's Journey/Change Arc

Protagonist Faces Problem

Call to Adventure

Beginning of Transformation

Mentor/Helper

Revelation

Transformation

Atonement

Return

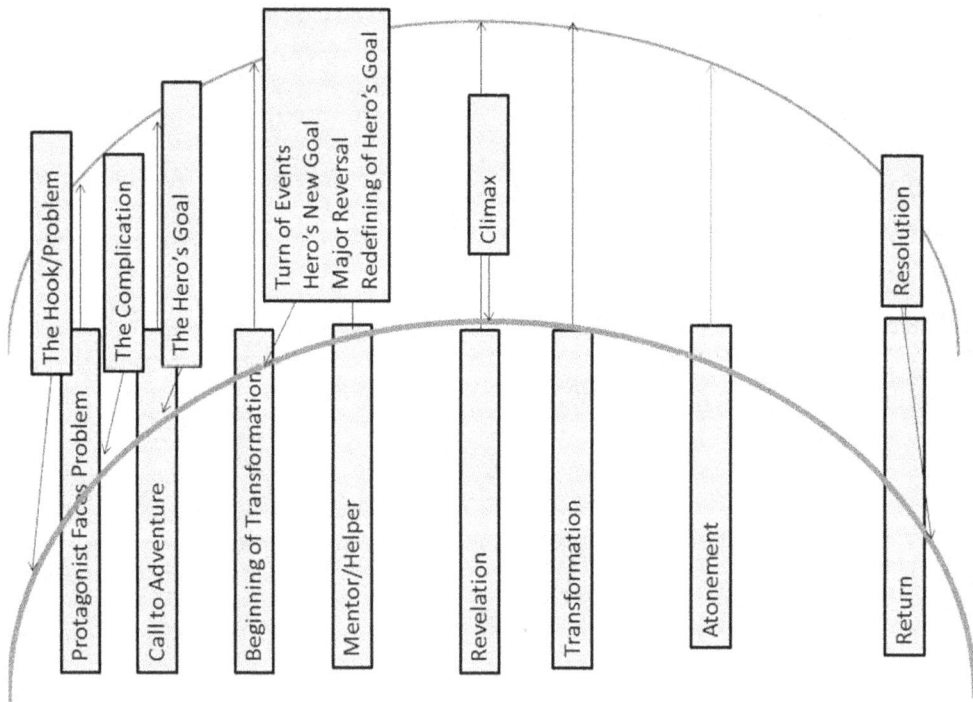

Hero's Journey and Plot Points

The Hook/Problem

The Complication

The Hero's Goal

Turn of Events
Hero's New Goal
Major Reversal
Redefining of Hero's Goal

Climax

Resolution

Protagonist Faces Problem

Call to Adventure

Beginning of Transformation

Mentor/Helper

Revelation

Transformation

Atonement

Return

The Growth and Shift Arc

The Growth Arc and the Shift Arc are grouped together, but have their own distinct arc. In the Growth Arc, the protagonist or hero or main character overcomes an internal opposition, which may actually be a weakness or fear. As he/she overcomes this internal opposition, he/she is also facing external opposition. Naturally, there is growth that results from these acts.

In the Shift Arc, the main character or protagonist or hero simply changes perspectives or learns different skills or gains a new role. Basically, there isn't a true change in the character; they are just using a different skill set. They don't overcome any internal obstacle; they don't become better than who they were. They just shift, instead of grow or change.

While this Character Arc seems to fall flat on the arc side, it is perfect for fast paced action novels or screenplays. In these stories where everything moves so quickly, it would be more difficult to move the *Main Character, Protagonist,* or *Hero* through a quest at the same time. Therefore, the *Growth and Shift Arc* serves a purpose in other types of stories.

Horror, thriller, some romance, and science fiction stories, as well as adventure stories need to have a quick pace throughout. The focus is more on plot than character. However, don't get too caught up in the plot that you don't give your characters enough attention. They still need to be well-rounded characters. The readers still need to identify with them in some way.

These are not the sort of stories that I write, so I don't have any examples to give within my own published works. We are familiar with these stories, such as the Indiana Jones movie series. The action keeps coming and coming; however, somehow the character makes it from beginning to end. Without a doubt, Indiana Jones remains Indiana Jones from start to end. His only quest is not his personal quest; instead it belongs to the plot.

Examining Indiana Jones gives us insight into the *Growth and Shift Arc,* because Indiana doesn't change. In some of these stories, especially when he seeks out the Holy Grail, Indiana does grow. He is forced into seeking out spiritual strength to find the Holy Grail; unfortunately many of the other characters in this movie story do not grow and meet their own death.

There is not much documentation for the Growth and Shift Arc. The basic points on the Growth/Shift Arc are:
- Protagonist Faces Problem
- Overcomes Internal Struggle/Change Perspective
- Faces External Opposition/Learns New Skills
- Begins Growth /Gains New Role
- Achieves Growth/Masters New Skills or Renews Talents
- Becomes Fuller, Better Person/Returns with Differences Acquired

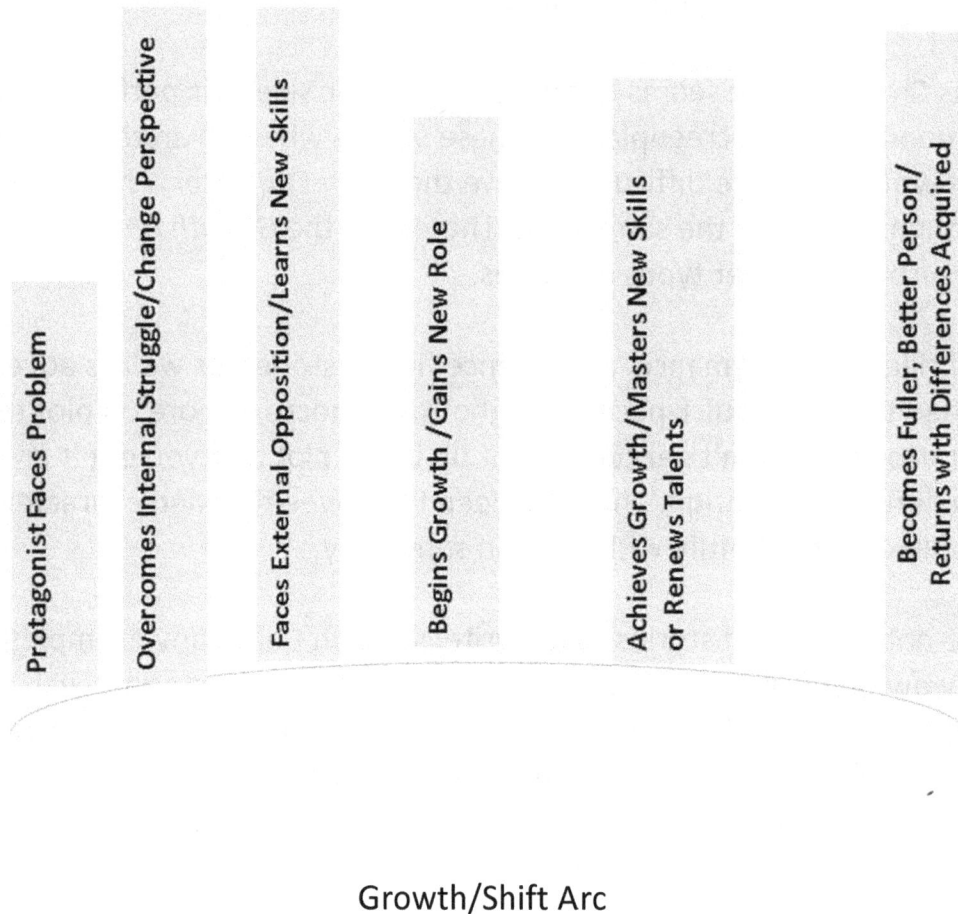

Protagonist Faces Problem

Overcomes Internal Struggle/Change Perspective

Faces External Opposition/Learns New Skills

Begins Growth /Gains New Role

Achieves Growth/Masters New Skills or Renews Talents

Becomes Fuller, Better Person/ Returns with Differences Acquired

Growth/Shift Arc

The Hook/Problem

The Complication

The Hero's Goal

Turn of Events
Hero's New Goal
Major Reversal
Redefining of Hero's Goal

Climax

Resolution

Protagonist Faces Problem

Overcomes Internal Struggle/ Change Perspective

Faces External Opposition/Learns New Skills

Begins Growth / Gains New Role

Achieves Growth/Masters New Skills or Renews Talents

Becomes Fuller, Better Person/ Returns with Differences Acquired

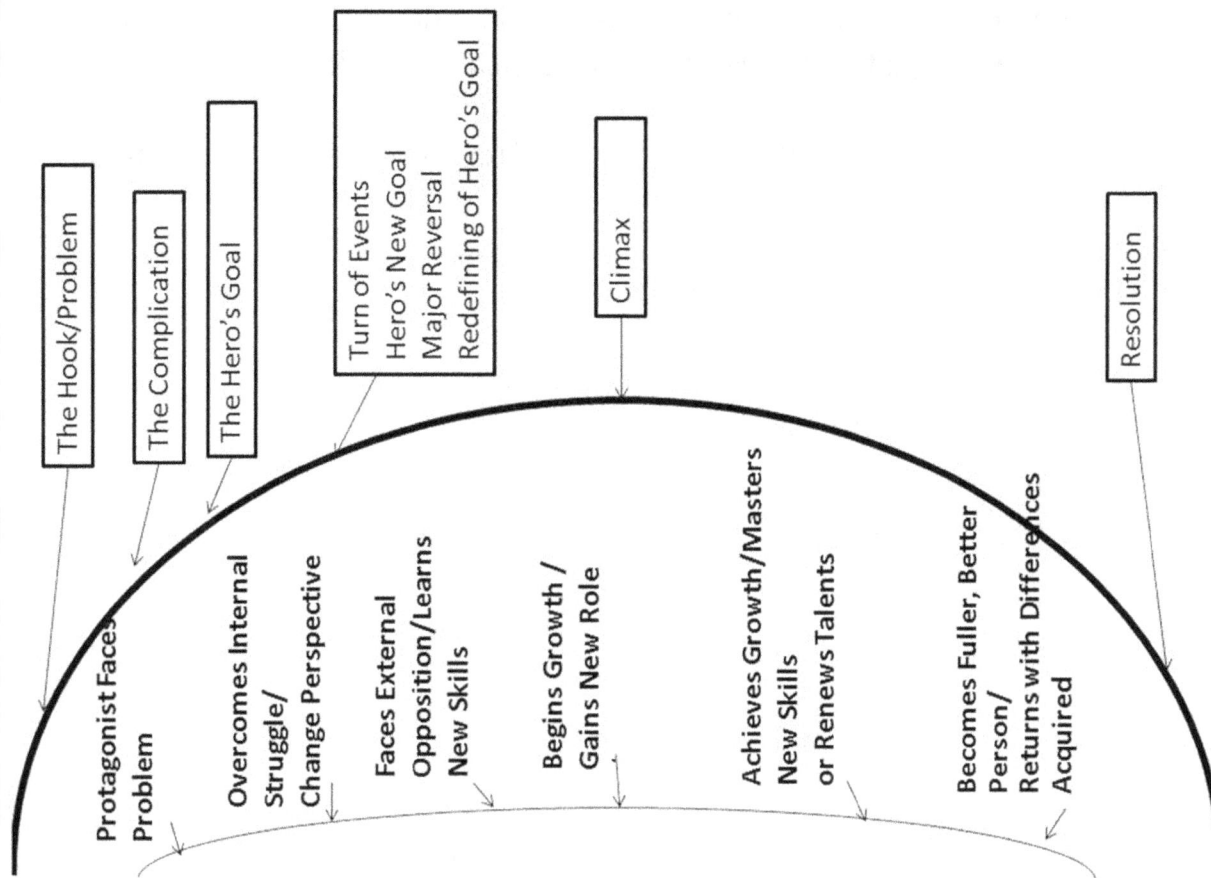

Growth/Shift Arc with Plot Points

The Fall Arc

The *Fall Arc* is our last example of character development through the study of character arcs. In this arc, we are introduced to the "tragedy." The character arc of the *Fall Arc* seems sad to me. On the Change Arc, the character arc makes a rainbow sort of arc. There is more of a flat arc on the *Growth and Shift Arc*. However with the *Fall Arc*, it takes the shape of an inverted arc. The *Protagonist, Main Character,* or *Hero* declines from the starting point. This character then becomes insane, immoral, or dead.

Since most of my fiction writing is children's books, I don't have any personal experience in writing a tragedy. Most of Shakespeare's works are tragedies.

There is not a lot of documentation on the Fall Arc; however, the basic Character Arc Points are:

- **Protagonist Faces Problem**
- **Discovers Problem with Self or Others**
- **Confronts Suspicions**
- **Sinks into Delusions**
- **Does Something Horrendous**
- **Protagonist Devastated**
- **Final Action –Protagonist Dies or Kills Someone**

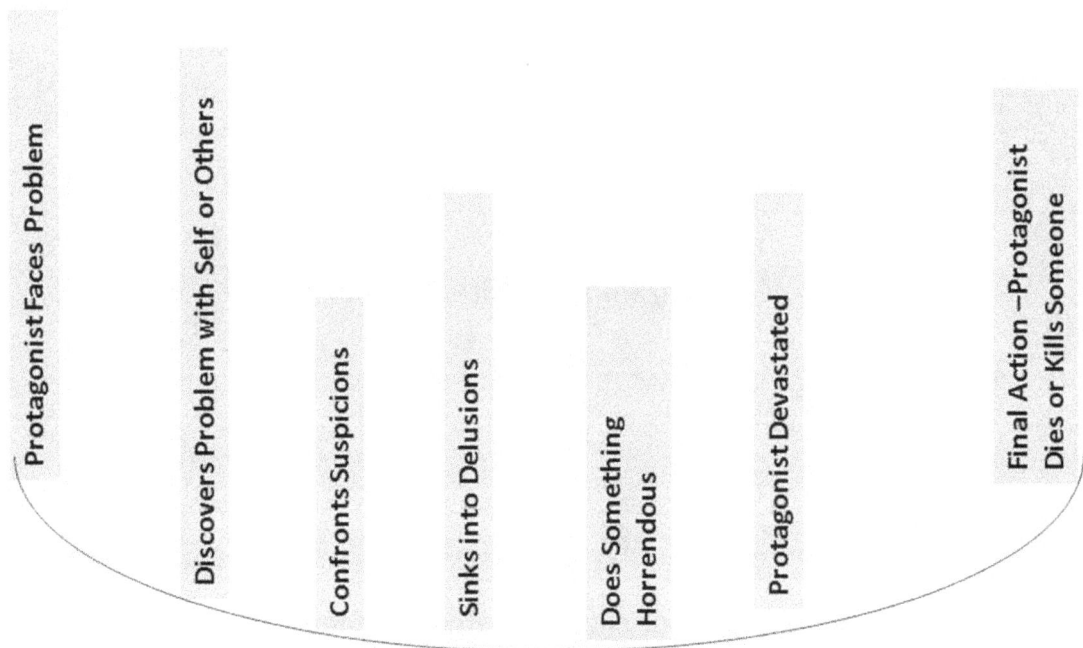

Protagonist Faces Problem

Discovers Problem with Self or Others

Confronts Suspicions

Sinks into Delusions

Does Something Horrendous

Protagonist Devastated

Final Action –Protagonist Dies or Kills Someone

Fall Arc

The Hook/Problem

Protagonist Faces Problem

The Complication

The Hero's Goal

Discovers Problem with Self or Others

Turn of Events
Hero's New Goal
Major Reversal
Redefining of Hero's Goal

Confronts Suspicions

Sinks into Delusions

Climax

Does Something Horrendous

Protagonist Devastated

Final Action –Protagonist Dies or Kills Someone

Resolution

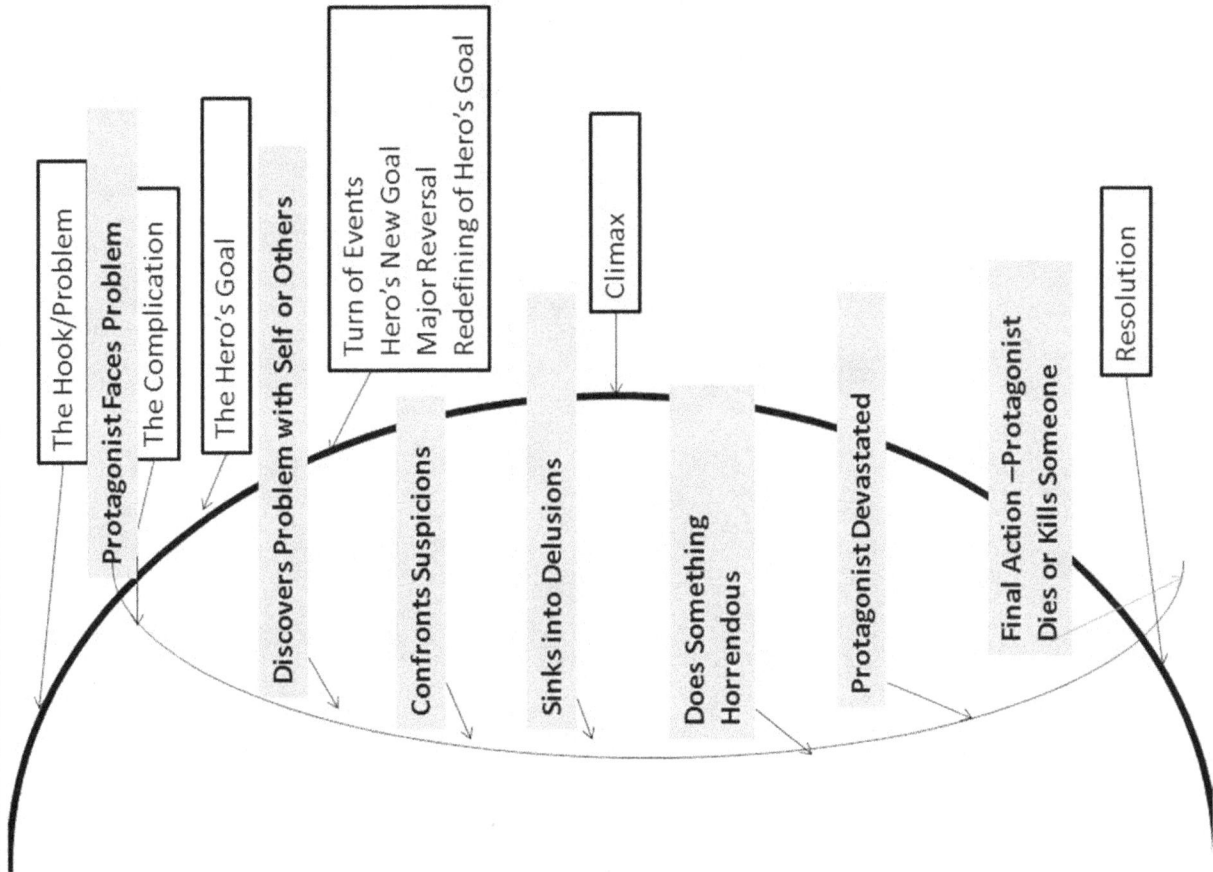

Fall Arc and Plot Points

Wrapping Up the Character Arcs

This brings us to the conclusion of Character Arcs. Although the information in this chapter can be helpful to the writer, it could just be more confusing. The bottom line on Character Arcs is how we choose which Character Arc to use. It is as simple as asking ourselves these two questions?

1. Where do you want the character to be at the end of your story?
2. Where does the character begin in your story?

There are many ways to work with characters; Character Arcs are just one way.

Character Secrets

What if your character had a secret?

The truth is that most characters have secrets. And that's very good for many stories. There may be some rules to follow when using secrets, such as:

- Your character's secret needs to belong in the story that you (the writer) are telling.
- The secret needs to be well-placed in the plot.
- This secret should not pull the reader out of the story.
- If the secret creates another story line, then it needs to be intentional and not just by chance.
- Your character's secret should reveal something about him/her that helps your reader understand the character better.
- This secret should not be something that doesn't already fit with your character, because it is part of the character and revealing a secret should add to the reader's knowledge of the character.
- This secret needs to be so important that it influence the outcome of the story. Think about it, if the secret doesn't move the story along, then it probably doesn't belong. And if you carefully craft the revelation of this secret, then it should impact all the characters, as well.
- After the secret is revealed, you should allow for all the other characters to react to the secret. Showing the other characters' emotions, whether they are angry, horrified, in tears, feel devastated, or simply crying helps to develop the other characters and should move the plot along.

"Revealing a character's secret(s) is always fun and exciting. You can't wait to drop the massive bombshell and mind-screw (yes, screw) your readers," says Darcy Pattison (http://www.darcypattison.com/characters/5-secrets-about-your-characters-secrets/). "There are a few ways I can think of how a writer can reveal a character's secrets:

- Let your character blurt it out! This is by far the easiest method and the one that will ensure the biggest shock to both your readers and your characters.

- Tell your readers, but keep the secret from the other characters and let them uncover it on their own. Don't forget to build the tension as the suspicious character comes closer to the truth.
- Draw it out. This method utilizes suspense and mystery, but it also takes the most work because neither the characters nor your readers know the secret. You can hint at a secret, but don't tell what it is until the perfect time comes for you to spill the beans, or for another character to uncover it."

Almost everyone in real life has secrets. Some are big and some are little. When you give a character a secret, it should be sizeable to fit the situation. I mean, come on, if this secret has to affect the whole outcome of this story, novel, or screenplay, it needs to be thought through well and I think "Colossal" would be the word to use. Naturally, your other characters might have secrets, as well.

Just like in life, all your characters keep something hidden, but as the writer, you need to figure out what their secrets are. They all desperately want to keep their secret hidden, who wouldn't?

Perhaps the easy thing is to learn what your characters' secrets are, and the tricky thing is how to reveal those secrets. Or, whether to reveal them at all!

While your job as the writer is to understand all the hidden secrets of all your characters, it doesn't mean you have to spill the beans on them! In fact, it might be better if you didn't reveal the secret. It could be fun, however, if these secrets were alluded to but not revealed.

Naturally, the plot of your story will help you decide whether any particular character needs to reveal his/her secret so that the story is resolved in the right manner. There are also some people who believe differently. You can keep the mystery in your story by extending the secret of a character(s) right to the end.

In real life, people have secrets. Sometimes they get revealed and sometimes they don't. I have known many lesbian women, who have lived with the secret of who they really were, but could not be public. In fact, one woman that I knew taught dance classes and was terrified that parents of her students would find out and not want their little girls to take dance from her. Living in the closet was difficult for her. Living through that era when being lesbian or gay could get you killed (don't even think about being trans) makes you appreciate the new open environment where same sex marriages are allowed. Knowing so many people who have been in love for 30 or more years and could finally get married makes my heart happy.

Just about everyone has a secret. I grew up in a dysfunctional family. My father had a drinking problem. He never admitted to being an alcoholic. We never talked about it in my family. It was a huge secret. It caused me a lot of pain when I was a teenager. I wasn't exactly the quiet type. I crossed my dad on a number of occasions. I even remember my mom and my sister helping me out my window, so I could go on a date.

You probably have some secrets. And maybe they are too personal or embarrassing to share. That's the way characters are...well, characters that we writers have done a good job creating in what we call three-dimensional characters. Two dimensional character or flat characters are not fully developed. We know little about them. These characters have a place in our stories, as well, but not as the *Protagonist* or the *Antagonist*.

Darcy Pattison writes about using the secret as a plot twist.(In a later chapter we will cover character and plot in a bit more depth.) "When we find out that Luke Skywalker's father is Darth Vader–the revelation twists the plot in a different direction. Make sure that the secret is truly hidden in the story as it develops, even as you prepare your readers for the revelation."

Source of Conflict–Making Sure the Secret Stays Secret
You see, a secret must really be secret, which often gives your story a bit conflict which you can exploit in your plot. Some secrets need to be tangible in that they need to have a physical presence.

Using some foreshadowing and breadcrumbs within your story, you can have the secret hidden yet still have a physical presence. For example, it can be a photo of someone that the secret surrounds; maybe a diary where the secret is written; a stack of letters from a secret lover; a magazine or newspaper clipping, which represents the person with whom the secret is shared; a favorite toy leftover from childhood that is the only memory of a favorite uncle; or a piece of clothing that you keep sealed away so that you can steal a feel and smell that reminds you of the mother who died so long ago.

Another way to use secrets in a powerful way is to wait for a big scene, especially the climax scene. Depending on the secret, of course, using the secret here might emphasize or give an extra twist to the clash between the *Protagonist* and the *Antagonist*.

When you, the writer, are developing your character(s) and giving them a secret, don't be shy about using one that actually comes from your own life. These tend to be more powerful, because you are intimately involved with this sort of secret.

Making Characters Real

Why do we want to make our characters real? The answer is probably quite apparent to you by now. If our characters are not real, our readers won't believe the story. They won't identify with the characters in the story and will stop reading.

It reminds me of the *Neverending Story*, when the Childlike Empress calls out to the Human Boy to give her a name. Bastian, the Human Boy, who is reading the story doesn't know that he is the one that can save the Childlike Empress. When he finally realizes what he needs to do, the Childlike Empress is barely alive. He calls out his mother's name and saves her. Then, Bastian enters the world of the story, Fantasia, and almost loses his memory of the real world.

The story drew Bastian into it and even into the world of Fantasia. The characters were real to Bastian, so much so that it became more real than the real world. Needless-to-say, the characters in the *Neverending Story* were real.

There are several ways to make your characters real:
- Draw on your own experience and the people around you.
- Build your character through Character Sketch Surveys.
- Map out character's arc.
- Give characters "secrets."
- Give them strengths and weaknesses.
- Do this for every character in your story.

Allowing your characters to be imperfect not only makes them more believable, it lets readers identify with them. The name of the game when creating characters is to make ones that your readers are going to care about.

Putting them into the plot and keeping your characters' personalities and names straight can sometimes be difficult when you first begin writing novels. Over time, you'll probably develop your own system.

My suggestion is to download the Character Sketch Survey files. These are located at: http://publishwithconnie.com/celebrity-confirm/ . There are three separate sketch surveys. Actually, there are two copies of each of the Character Sketch Surveys so that you can choose between a *Word doc file* or a *PDF file*. I often like to keep everything on my computer rather than in a binder. You do not need do all three. You just need the one you like best.

If you are writing a novel and really need an in-depth profile, the Character Sketch Survey – 2 is probably what you want. If you want a quicker and less-detailed profile of your character, then either Character Sketch Survey– 1 or Character Sketch Survey – 3 will probably do the job.

I suggest printing out the Character Sketch Survey. If you aren't sure, download them all, print them all. Look them over and make a decision. You should download one for each character in your book, so that you understand who your characters are. For minor characters, I would choose one of the shorter surveys.

Print out a Character Sketch Survey for each character in your book, put it all into a 3-ring binder. This way when you are half-way through your book and cannot remember the right name for a character or what they look like, you'll have it at your fingertips.

Before you embark on your journey of writing your book, you may want to create all your characters. While this chapter is about making your characters real, you also have to make your characters distinguishable. If all of your characters are alike, your readers will get confused.

Creating a Character Sketch Survey for each character helps you prevent a lot of rewriting. One of my students is writing a middle grade fantasy novel series. She began writing before she did the Character Sketch Surveys. But she stopped writing and took some time organizing, which included writing a survey for each character. She discovered that she had given the same name to two of her characters. She also found that some of the names were too similar.

In some of my own work, I have noticed that when similar names are used confusion happens. When writing for children, this happens more often. Even names that begin with the same phonetic sounds can be confusing. This is just as important for adult fiction; we just usually don't focus on that as much.

There are several ways to avoid creating similar sounding names. The first way is to simply fill out one of the three Character Sketch Surveys. Keep those sheets handy in a three-ring binder while you are writing. This allows you to thumb through to check on a character. Not only will you see if you've used similar names, but it also keeps you from creating similar characters using duplicate characteristics.

Another simple method is to write down a list from A to Z, marking off letters that you've used. This works well, if you can keep up with your list, and if you don't need to worry about creating similar characters through re-using similar characteristics.

You might also create a system using two lists of A to Z. This helps you by allowing you to mark off first name and last name letters. This is a helpful method of keeping track of your name choices. However, if you also need or want to keep track of further characteristics, the survey method would work best. On the other hand, the alphabetical listing is so simple compared to flipping through several pages of character sketch surveys.

It is usually my recommendation to go with the simplest solutions. However, novelists often have numerous characters in their books. If juggling characters sounds like more work than you think you can handle in your head, then creating the surveys might be a better solution

Creating realistic characters also requires that you study other people and how they move, dress, etc. There are some great places to "people watch." The mall is always a good place, but don't overlook the local coffee shop.

Remember, "People-Watching" falls into research, so keep track of mileage. If you eat out, you might spend a few minutes looking at the people in the restaurant and notice family interaction. Think about the characters you are preparing for your book or that you have created.

Often, writers will keep "People" notes filed away for further use. So when you are doing your "People-Watching," take good notes. It's probably not a good idea to write them down in the restaurant, unless you are eating alone. Your table partners could get perturbed if you are watching other people and not paying any attention to them.

Roles and Character

Within any story you have both roles and characters. The characters are not any more synonymous with their roles than we are in real life. We all play roles, some of us have multiple roles. This can link back to our archetypes, which are pretty, much shell characters. However, they are often like the old nursery rhyme: the butcher, the baker, and the candlestick maker. These don't necessarily define who we are.

I have worn many hats in my life. I've been the mother, the dance mom, the gymnastic mom, the soccer mom, the baseball mom, the football mom, the cheerleader mom, the wife, the girlfriend, the writer, the poet, the student, the chamber member, and probably more. We each have a long list of roles that we either currently play or have played.

I am a mother and that label tends to be for life, yet, "mother" does not define all that I am. Nor do any of the other roles that I have played in my life. Even as writer or author, this is only one aspect of who we are. Just like our own lives, our characters play roles within the story that we write.

At the end of the story, do we know everything about any one of our characters? My answer would be, "No." As a writer, we must know everything we can about our characters from what their favorite color is to what their sexual preferences are. Our knowing this character still does not mean that we can push all of this knowledge into one story, one novel, or one screenplay. We try to share as much as is relevant to our story.

If we are writing a story about Captain Mike, we are likely to share all of who he is when he is the captain of his ship. We might share other aspects if it is relevant to our story. If the story doesn't involve his family arrangement, then we might not even reveal this role.

Why? The information that we share about our character needs to be relevant and move our story forward. Do we need to know that Captain Mike was born premature? Probably not!

We rarely start stories with "Once upon a time..." or "He was born on a dark and stormy night on the banks of the Mississippi. His Poppa said that he was too small and wouldn't last the night. Yet, now he is Captain Mike."

If the fact that he was born on the banks of the Mississippi and was premature furthers our story, we might include this information, but is it a good opening? Probably, not!

So Captain Mike plays the role of a captain of a ship. He might also be a father. He might also have been born premature. He might also have been born on the banks of the Mississippi. He might also have been a church going boy. He might have been a choir member. He might even have mowed the lawn. But if our story is set on the high seas, these other roles are meaningless to our story.

They are not meaningless to us as authors. We need to know these details to understand who Captain Mike was and is. We want to know everything about our character, but we probably aren't going to share all we know.

Like in real life, it is also possible that our story about Captain Mike might show many other roles that he plays. As the captain of his ship, he might also be the counselor, the peacemaker, the adventurer, and more. If our story is about Captain Mike on the high seas, we might actually show him in these roles rather than starting from the moment he was born. Unless, of course, if the story requires us to know this about Captain Mike.

Roles and characters are closely woven into most stories. We don't see just the role of a person in real life, nor do we within our stories. The phrase of "weaving stories" has been used since ancient times. It is a good metaphor for how stories come together. We weave what we know about the role of our *Protagonist* and *Antagonist* with relevant plot details, plus descriptions of who these people are. We share insight into our character often through hearing the thoughts of our character. In real life, we rarely pay attention to our own thoughts as we move through a plot point. Of course, our lives have plot points! But we often don't see them in this way.

Character and Point of View

When we think of character in a story, we think of the "Hero's Journey," which we addressed in the "Character Arc." When we think of *Point of View (POV),* we equate that with story development rather than character development.

However, with a whole cast of characters, you also have a whole cast of POVs. As the author, we need to tell the story as we believe it would best be told. Many authors, including myself, don't just write words on paper/screen, we see it and hear it, as if we were watching a movie. It is through this lens that the author can determine the best POV.

It's possible to envision some piece of the story from all POVs, and then you know for sure who should be telling this story. The goal is to gain the attention of readers from the very first word. While it may seem like an impossible goal, the POV becomes clearer as the author works with his/her cast of characters and listens to what they each want to offer. Each cast member has a piece of the story to reveal, but the POV relies on the author to determine.

You see, the story is not the same from the POV of each character. In reality, only one POV can tell the story that the author wants to tell. While there may be more than the three POVs that I will be listing here, I'm sharing with you what English literature scholars' have settled on.

First Person:

This is one of my personal favorites. This POV comes from one character who tells the story through his/her POV. In this story, this character is recognized by the use of "I," "Me," "My" or "Mine." From this POV, we not only get the story narrated from this POV, but we also are given access to all the thoughts of this character. We literally see the world through this character's eyes, ears, and mind.

The limitation of this POV is that we can only see and hear through this one character's POV. We cannot even know all of this person's thoughts in the same way that we know ourselves. We aren't always completely transparent in revealing all of our inner selves.

The Role of the *Reader* is to go beyond what the narrator says. One of the classic ways to demonstrate this comes from "To Kill a Mockingbird." The POV is a young child named Scout, who doesn't understand the complexities of the world, such as race and socio-economic relations. As an innocent child, however, Scout gives enough information that allows the reader to "read" between the lines and go beyond what the young girl can explain. Perhaps, one of the things that endears us to this story is Scout's honest and simple world view. She has no understanding beyond what is fair and what is not fair. In contrast, we see through Scout's naivety how other characters rationalize the inequity of justice.

Second Person:

This is a difficult POV for most to grasp, in part, because it is fairly rare. This is when the author speaks directly to the reader. You see this when the author makes use of "you" and "your."

For example, this book is mostly written this way with the occasional addition of "I" where personal example was needed. The *Second Person POV* is more often used in non-fiction educational materials. Some authorities boldly say that the *Second Person* is so rare that when you come across it, you should pay attention. This is considered a daring choice with specific purposes.

What happens with *Second Person* is that the reader becomes an active participant in the story. In this book, an example of *Second Person* is, "Whether **your** character is the main character or a minor character, the reader cannot see what is not written on the pages."

Most of my educational material is written in *Second Person*. However, all my fiction work is done in *First Person*.

Third Person:

The *Third Person POV* is done from an omniscient narrator. This narrator knows what all the characters are thinking. It is sort of the outside person looking into the story, almost like a newscaster, but one that can magically know what everyone is thinking, as well as saying. This gives the reader the widest look at the story. The negative of this POV is that it can feel impersonal.

The *Third Person POV* can also be done with a limited view. Whereas; the all-knowing narrator knows the thoughts of every character, the limited narrator knows only the thoughts of one character.

At first glance, you may think that instead of using the limited narrator, you might as well do *First Person*. But there is a big difference, because *First Person* is from one character's POV rather than from the author's voice as the narrator or storyteller.

As a writer, I prefer to write in *First Person* when writing fiction, especially children's stories. When writing non-fiction, I prefer the *Second Person*. None of these POVs is better than the other. I firmly believe that the POV is dictated by the story you want to write.

Character and Plot

Every story has both a *Character* and a *Plot*. Most stories have more than one *Character*. Some stories may have more than one *Plot*, but this is rare.

Character needs *Plot* to tell a story. And *Plot* needs *Character* to tell a story. So these two items are basically married to make a story. The *Plot* can be mapped out with *Plot Points*, which are basically the bare bones structure of the *Plot*

There are many variations of what are and are not Plot Points. While this chapter is not a study on Plot Points, we need to have that bare bones structure so we can then plug our Character's Arc Points into the Story Plot Points. Once you've done this, you have successfully mapped out your story.

Stories have a beginning, middle and end. However, we can further break that down into a Five-Point Plot Analysis:

1. The Hook/Problem: This is an introduction of a problem or conflict that is basic to the entire story. This is the conflict that slowly plays out and is resolved in some manner by the end of the play, screenplay, novel or story. This needs to be compelling and draw the audience into the story; otherwise, there would be no need to write the story.

EXAMPLE: Mary hits Sally in the middle of the mall.

2. The Complication: This is where the original conflict described in *The Hook* gets more complicated.

EXAMPLE: We learn that Sally went out with Mary's boyfriend.

3. The Hero's Goal: At this stage of the story, the goal of the hero has been clearly defined and the hero is clearly setting out to achieve it.

EXAMPLE: We know that Mary is out to win back her boyfriend and see her working toward this goal.

POINTS IN BETWEEN
- **Turn of Events:** *The hero now has an obstacle to overcome.*
- **Hero's New Goal:** The hero now establishes a new goal.
- **Major Reversal:** *The hero appears to have lost all goals.*
- **Redefining of Hero's Goal:** *Hero must redefine goal into what showdown is about.*

4. Climax: This point is the highest point in the story.

EXAMPLE: Mary sees Sally. They reminisce about the dead boyfriend.

5. Resolution: This is the very last scene where all the loose ends get tied up. Whatever needs to be resolved gets resolved at this point.

EXAMPLE: Mary and Sally become best friends and move into an apartment together.

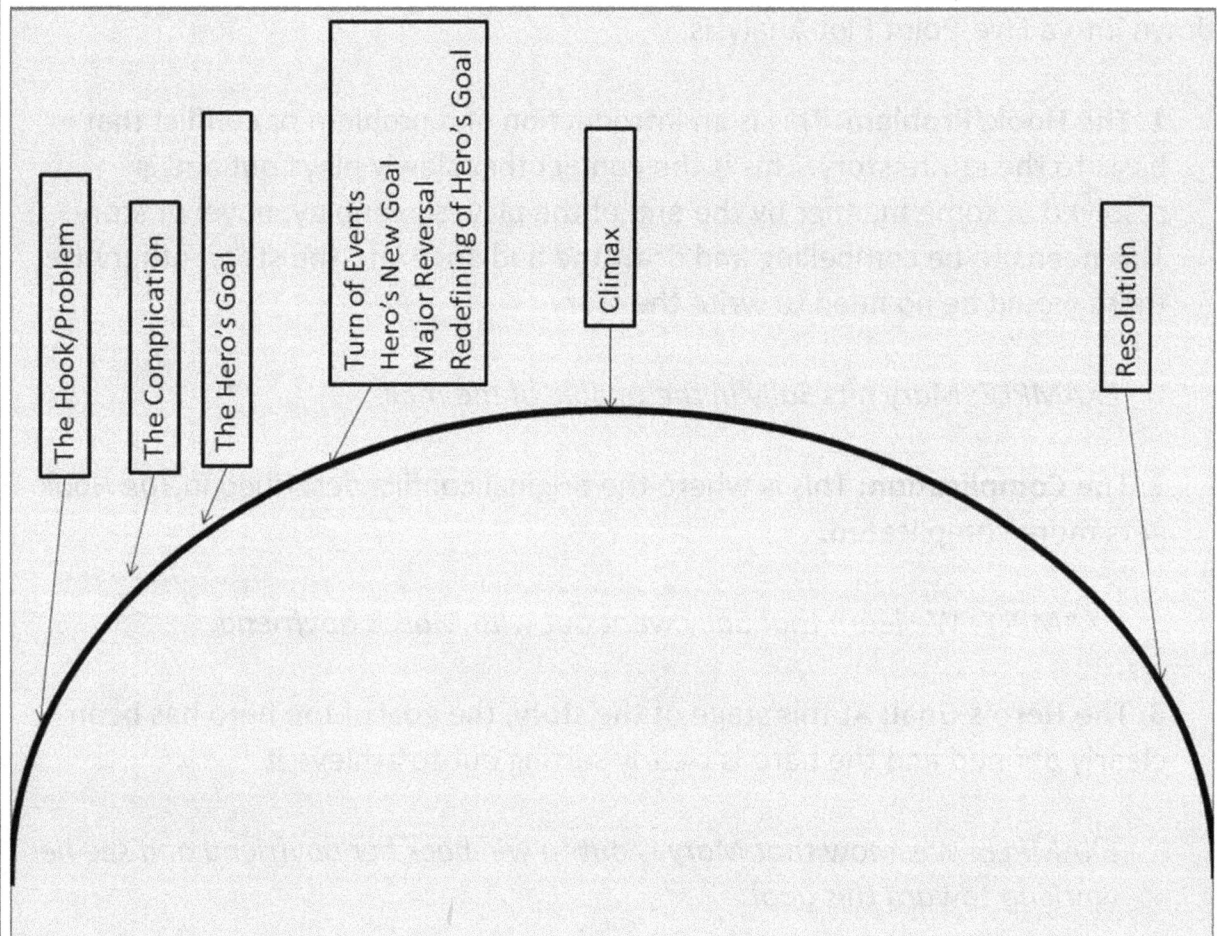

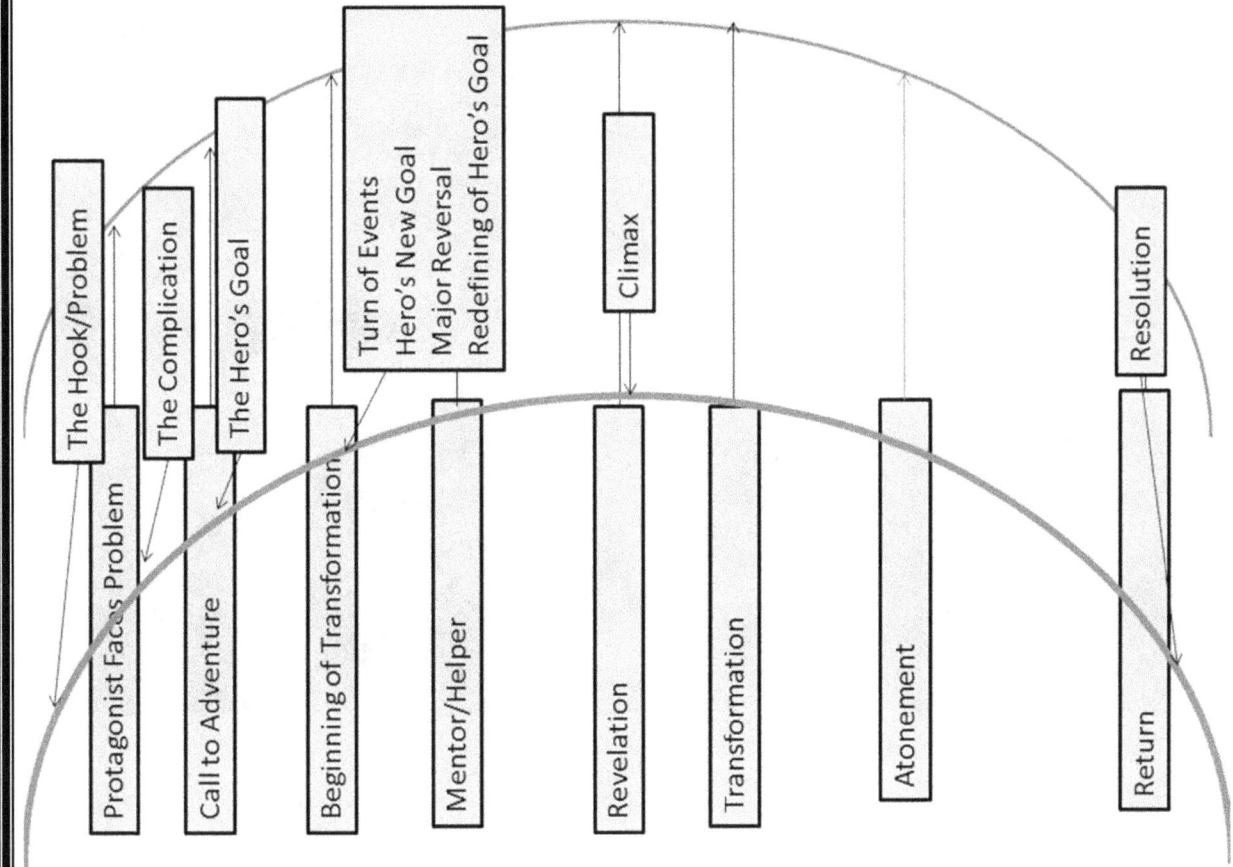

The Hook/Problem

Protagonist Faces Problem

The Complication

Call to Adventure

The Hero's Goal

Beginning of Transformation

Turn of Events
Hero's New Goal
Major Reversal
Redefining of Hero's Goal

Mentor/Helper

Climax

Revelation

Transformation

Atonement

Resolution

Return

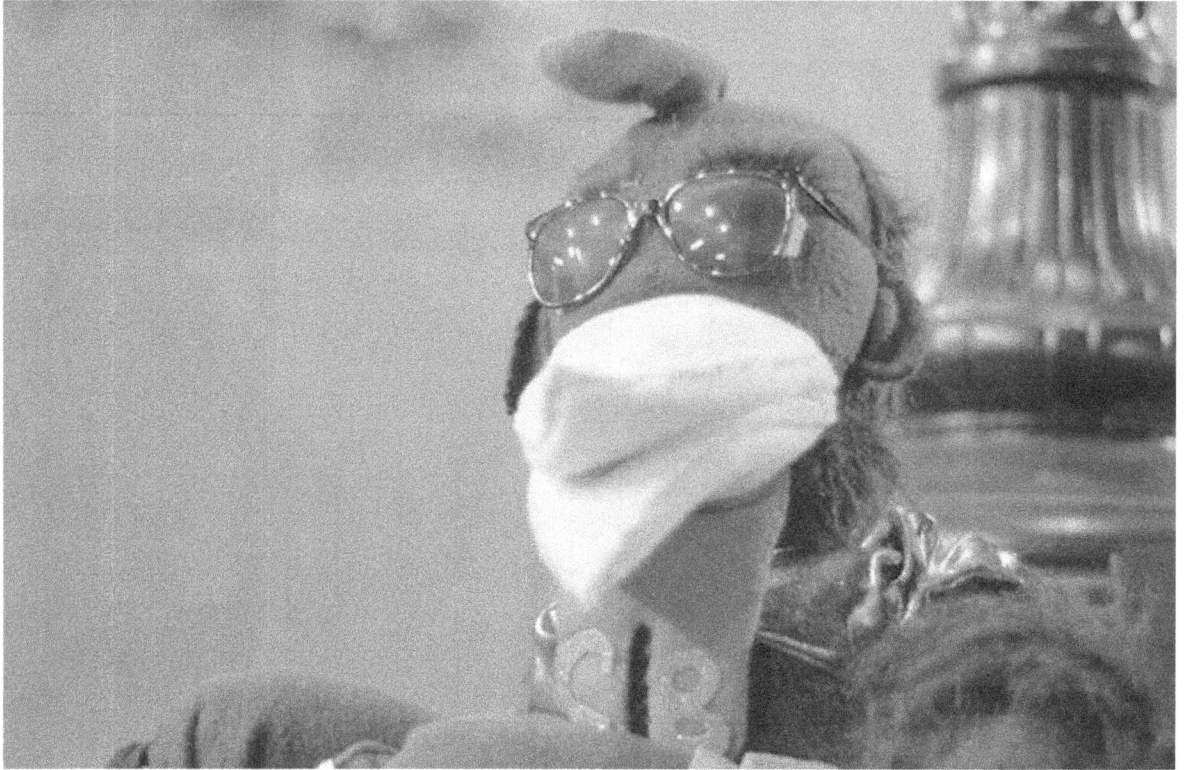

Character Development and Troubleshooting

Flat Characters

Flat Characters need to be blown up. No! Not with dynamite! Blow them up with substance. Give your characters a few problems, maybe a secret, as well. Go back to your Character Sketch Survey and fill in some details.

Holly Lisle in "Create a Character Clinic" says, "Characters do not form in the moments when we're happy. Characters form when things begin to go wrong."

It's true. Think about a child who lives in a loving family and pretty much all his/her needs are met. Everything in the child's life is basically perfect. The first time any problem comes up, this child will have no idea what to do.

When I adopted my son, I remember the caseworker telling me that it was good that we had not grown up in "perfect" families and that we had gone through some adversities in our lives. In her eyes, we were then ready to raise our adopted child, who came to us with many layers of issues.

So, the fix for a FLAT Character is to blow them up with adversity, fears, likes, dislikes and really find out who your character is. It doesn't matter whether this character is your main character/protagonist, antagonist or an insignificant character in your cast; create a Character Sketch Survey for each character. Print it out and put it in a binder. Refer to it each time you begin to write about that character. Insignificant characters may not have as much back story.

Characters Aren't Coming Alive

Characters do not come alive if they aren't believable. The way to make characters come alive is to develop your character using a Character Sketch Survey, so that you understand your character completely.

Understand where this character fits into your story. If your main character isn't coming alive on your pages, then you haven't done your job to develop the character with all sorts of back story information. If your character is well-developed and you put them into the plot for your story, then they will come alive.

Sins of Characterization

There are many sins surrounding characterization. Probably the biggest sin is creating a character that is too convenient, too over-used. If you are new to the genre for which you are writing, then do your homework: read. Actually, that also applies to seasoned writers who get too complacent in their own work. You need to read within your own genre. Put this into your calendar. You should schedule time for reading just as you should schedule time for writing.

If you are having trouble with characterization, you should probably spend more time developing your characters. Using the Character Sketch Surveys provided in this book and available for download on my publishwithconnie.com site can be a good start.

Characters Not Memorable

When writers tell me that their characters are not memorable, I wonder how they are developing their characters. Finding and developing memorable characters means that your character and your plot fit together. For example, a cowboy in a story set in New York City might be hard to pull off, unless there is a real good reason for him/her to be there.

Usually this means that you, the writer, have not spent enough time developing your character. The key to making memorable characters is making them realistic. It's hard to remember characters that you cannot identify with.

Naturally, another issue to examine is your audience. I primarily write children's stories, but if I bring in an adult character, it's pretty likely that my audience wouldn't be able to connect. If that adult character is a grandfather and the story is about a boy and his grandfather, then there's a good chance that boys will connect with this story. Girls might not, but a story about a grandfather and grandson should have no expectations that girls will connect with such a story.

I may sound like a broken record here, but characters that aren't memorable might also be characters that are not well-developed. Go back to your Character Sketch Survey.

Characters that Melt into a Puddle and Now You're in a Muddle

I hate when that happens! Really! It's so messy on the paper...or in my computer!

When you have a character that just falls apart somewhere in your story, then your character probably hasn't been developed well or your plot has some issues. The first thing that I would do, not surprisingly, is to go back to the Character Sketch Survey. Chances are good that you need to spend more time developing your character.

When a character melts into a puddle, it usually means that you didn't know how the character would act in the plot situation. Again, the Character Sketch Survey is an easy way to put more character into your character.

This is not a complete guide to everything that might go wrong with your character. Obviously, my recommendation for whatever ails a character is to return to the Character Sketch Survey.

Each of the three Character Sketch Surveys are available for download at http://publishwithconnie.com/characters. There is also a free introductory course: Character Development 101. After you have completed Character Development 101, you are invited to do Character Development 201, and then 301 and 401.

About the Author

Connie Dunn is an author, speaker, educator and owner of Publish with Connie and Nature Woman Wisdom Press. She writes courses, such as her signature, "12 Easy Steps to Publishing," children's books, such as her collection of children's stories, "A Spider, Some Thread, and a Labyrinth Walk," and non-fiction, such as "12 Steps to Publishing: Workbook," "Press Releases Made Easy." She has more than 25 years of experience in writing for magazines and newspapers. She had a regular column in the Dallas Morning News, which focused on small and home-based businesses. For this column, she won an award from the SBA (Small Business Administration). Connie also developed courseware for a number of start-up technology firms.

She worked with publishers, such as Prentice Hall and Taylor Publishing as a Developmental (content) Editor. She self-published her first book in 1981, and developed a collection of stories with a collaborator in the 1990s. She writes children's books, non-fiction, and fiction. Connie believes that everyone has a book in them and her greatest joy is in traveling with her students on their writing journeys.

Connie lives in Franklin, MA, with her wife Joyce, their five-and-a-half-pound Chihuahua named Rusty, and plus-sized cat named Sophie.

The End